CONTENTS

INTRODUCTION

In my first book *Becoming Toxic People's Worst Nightmare: Learn how to set boundaries and stop anyone from mistreating you* I explained toxic people's behavior and tried to help you understand it to defeat it. I didn't, however, provide specific advice about what to do; I rather tried to provide you with enough knowledge to help you develop your own plan of action and choose your own behavior. And I still believe in that. I believe you should have the right mentalities and then the right behaviors and actions will start manifesting themselves in your life.

In this book, the advice is more practical. In fact, I started writing it as a workbook. You will find practical things to say and do to toxic people in different situations and contexts. However, when I say "practical" I don't mean that I will just tell you to go and do X. I will explain why you should do X and what mentalities toxic people have and what you should do about that. That is more powerful than blindly following a piece of advice.

We will look at specific toxic behaviors and how to handle them. We will also consider specific situations where you are likely to get sucked into a toxic dynamic and help you not to. And overall, we will try to instill mentalities and ways of acting that will help you become a more emotionally healthy person.

The book is structured this way:

- **PART ONE:** Okay, warm up with these small nuggets.
- **PART TWO:** Let's get deep.
- **PART THREE:** Let's reach that deep point where the real wounds are.
- **PART FOUR:** Let's talk about what is healthy!

Each part will have a brief description of how it can help you and what you can expect. Combining them together, you will have the ability to really become *Toxic People's Worst Nightmare*. But I don't think you want that. I think you want to become more emotionally healthy and stable and have relationships that reflect that. This is a side benefit you will get as well if you are willing to apply what you are about to learn.

In a hindsight, this is a short book that will not take much time to read. However, I do invite you to read it carefully. Just because It's short doesn't mean it's an easy read. And just because you can easily and quickly read it doesn't mean you fully understand it.

Happy read! I wish you find your answers and more.

Mosab Alkhteb

1st of December, 2020

PART ONE

Those are simple, yet effective, pieces of advice to handle different toxic situations. They are not so deep, yet are effective at making you a more assertive person. Assertiveness is the number one trait you need to handle toxic people.

STOP TRYING TO SAVE THEM; STOP TRYING TO CHANGE THEM.

There's this idea of the drama triangle. Drama needs certain ingredients to exist and operate. The drama triangle is when there's a victim, a predator, and a savior. Those are three roles that we all can play at times. They can be dangerous when we get sucked in playing them.

The victim is someone who relinquishes their responsibility for saving themselves. A predator can be real (person/people) or it can be in the form of oppressive situations. The savior is the person who attempts to save the victim.

However, the victim doesn't want to be helped. They want to be saved. The difference is huge. Those who want help will be helping themselves. But those who want to be saved are toxic. They don't want to do the work. They don't want to sacrifice what they have for what they can get. And the idea of being responsible for their lives isn't exactly exciting to them. And even if they are saved, there's no shortage of predators in life. It's just a matter of time before another catastrophe befalls them. And it's not healthy to always be saved instead of developing your own strength to help yourself out. Giving up your personal responsibility is equivalent to giving up your personal power and strength.

But not all victims want to be saved. Some want to stay where they are although they are in a shithole. Why is that? Because there are secondary benefits and privileges to being a victim. Those benefits and gains come at a high cost, but playing the victim role is about being okay with paying those high costs. As a victim, you don't have to do anything. You don't have to shoulder any responsibilities. After all, you are a victim! And you can easily get attention and sympathy. People will find you excuses and not expect much of you. For a while, you can get away with some stuff and not be held accountable. The biggest price you pay, however, is your personal strength. Anything can level you and take you out.

Now, the toxicity of the victim isn't what I want to discuss at this point. I am not trying to educate you about the victim's mentality to help you get rid of it. What I want to warn against is the tendency to try to save the victim and then getting sucked into the role f the savior. That's not only a losing battle but also a toxic dynamic that's a hallmark for a toxic relationship.

Toxic people can come in the cute shape of a victim. And you might want to save them and end up not only disappointing and hurting yourself, but also you will make your life and theirs worse. Yours by fighting a losing battle and draining yourself. Theirs by enabling them and taking some of their responsibility from them.

Some toxic people can play the victim role very well. They are always in pain and are suffering. Yet, they are not able to make use of any piece of advice. Even saving them doesn't seem to be working. It's just a matter of time before another catastrophe befalls them. And somehow, it's all out of their control and there's nothing they can do. Even your good suggestions about what you think they should do seem to be worthless. So, you sometimes end up doing the work for them or finding excuses for why they can't do the work themselves. And they just keep spiraling downwards, despite your 'genuine' attempts to help them spiral upwards and have a good life. Or they just keep treating you poorly because they can't do better.

I am not against helping other people when they are struggling. But there's a difference between trying to help someone and trying to save them. If someone refuses to be helped, stop helping them. If someone doesn't want to change despite their shitty situation, stop offering help.

It becomes bloody toxic when you are trying to save someone from their deepest shitholes against their will.

It's like trying to change someone. It never works. The desire to change has to come from within; otherwise, it is manipulated and not genuine and therefore won't last.

Stop enabling them by excusing their obviously demoralizing behavior. Stop offering them help when they won't take it. Stop taking their own responsibilities as your own. Stop trying to change them. And for god's sake, keep in my mind how difficult it is to change your own self, let alone others.

And oh, stop getting your sense of importance from feeling deeply needed by somebody else! That's toxic, too. You will live your life putting off fires and putting up with unnecessary drama.

RECOGNIZE THE USELESS, SUCKING CONVERSATIONS THEY TRY TO HAVE WITH YOU AND DON'T PARTICIPATE.

What's the purpose of having a conversation?

And what makes a good conversation?

A conversation is a dialogue, a discussion, and a way to orient/reorient our thoughts and feelings.

A good conversation is one in which you are oriented properly as a result of the quality of the discussion and the dialogue.

That is, a conversation that makes you a better person. It doesn't necessarily mean that it makes you feel better. Some are actually hard and heavy. But the final result is your betterment.

So, all in all, a conversation is just a tool that can make you either a better person or a worse one. There's a reason therapy exists! Therapy is just an attempt to have a conversation that will hopefully unlock and untie something within you, as far as I am concerned. And that can't happen with low-quality conversations. In fact, low-quality conversations can be the reason we need therapy; they can be the reason we get hurt and have wounds all over our emotional bodies. Think of abuse. Think of all the psychological issues that can arise thanks to the malevolent conversations we engage in.

Don't underestimate the power of words.

So, the useless, sucking conversations are the ones that drag you down.

And toxic people usually engage in such conversations. Why? Because they are *easily* able to engage in low-quality, toxic discussions and dialogues (well, usually monologues, to be honest). Why? Because those toxic discussions and monologues match the toxicity that is present in their thoughts, feelings, and beliefs. And, not surprisingly, those conversations have the negative outcome of disorienting and troubling you.

Don't engage. Don't participate. Ignore. Ignore more.

Usually, toxic people will try to provoke you. They will try to engage in these types of conversations. Some of them have nothing to lose.

But you do. And there's nothing to gain. Choose your sanity; pick your battles carefully. And remember this. The quality of the conversations you have has a great impact on the quality of your life.

(Note: the quality of the conversation is about how much truth each individual is telling.)

USE CONDITIONS TO ARTICULATE YOUR BOUNDARIES.

Making your boundaries clear, without imposing them onto others, is what assertiveness is.

Being an articulate person is a blessing. It's so powerful. And there's a little difference between being assertive and being articulate. A person who is articulate is most likely an assertive person who sets strong and clear boundaries. A person who is not able to articulate their thoughts and feelings and ideas will have a hard time setting and enforcing boundaries as well.

I am not going to talk about being an articulate person, for that's too big a topic to be discussed here. But I will talk about one small tip that will help you become a bit more articulate.

Let's start right at the beginning.

Some people don't have their boundaries clearly articulated nor defined. Not only to other people but also to themselves. They are not aware of their boundaries and therefore they have weak ones.

After all, if you don't know what you are willing to accept and what not, you are more likely to accept about anything!

One of the simplest ways you can start articulating your boundaries is by using conditions.

If X, then Y.

And I don't mean that you go out there telling people that if they did X, then you would do Y. No! Though you can do it, it can be awkward sometimes.

You need to be using those conditions to be aware of your own boundaries.

If someone is behaving foolishly or arrogantly around you, you are not interested in being their friend; you will just shrug them off and move on. If someone doesn't respect your time, you politely tell them to; if they still don't listen, you stop hanging out with them. If someone is rude, you have no time or respect for them. You move on.

You get the idea. The idea behind conditions is helping you become aware of your boundaries and articulating them. And it's a good way to know if a boundary is being pushed and violated.

The condition is the trigger. It's how you know if someone stepped on the line.

Of course, you set these conditions based on your own values. For instance, if you value honesty and someone lied to you and betrayed you, you would not excuse their behavior nor justify it and you would stop hanging out with them. If you value respect, you are not willing to tolerate disrespectful behavior. You can choose to walk away or to minimize contact with the disrespectful person or to confront them. The disrespectful behavior is the trigger.

So, using conditions can be a good idea to become aware of your values and therefore set boundaries around them. From there, you will be telling your mind that if someone did X, you must do Y. And you stick to doing that. Furthermore, it can be a good way to let people know what you will not tolerate and what lines they shouldn't cross. Let them know of the consequences. That's called enforcing your boundaries. Do keep in mind, however, that some people will still push your boundaries even when you explicitly set them and articulate them. The solution is very simple: walk your talk. They won't believe you are serious about the said boundary until you actually do what you say you are going to do.

Nothing screams assertiveness more than articulated

boundaries. And conditions are the fastest and quickest way to articulate where the line on the sand is drawn and what will happen should it be crossed.

DON'T DEFEND YOURSELF OR JUSTIFY ANYTHING.

Here's a little trick to help you win arguments.

Attacking is better than defending *when you are sure the other person is just out to get you.* In other words, don't justify yourself or defend your situation when someone is only interested in tearing you down.

Instead, attack.

When you try to defend or justify, you are taking yourself to a corner where you can be easily defeated. They want you to go there because there they can beat the hell out of you. Let me explain. Their accusations and attacks direct the conversation towards a place where they have more power than you. And once you start going in that direction, by justifying and defending yourself, you are already in the wrong neighborhood.

Don't go there in the first place. Stay right where you are. The fact that they want to take the fight to another neighborhood should be enough evidence that they are less powerful right here.

Stay where you are and get leverage. Or play their same game and direct the conversation towards a place where you have more power.

This means attacking. Attacking usually means bringing the focus back to the bully and their flaws. *Shed a light on one of their flaws instead of defending yours.* And if you can't think of a flaw they have, here are a few: the fact that they are trying to project their own insecurities onto you. The fact that they are trying to boost their ego by picking up on others. Or maybe the fact that they want attention. Anyway, don't defend and do tell them to go and get a life! Yes, you can use this phrase. It works so long you keep the focus on them instead of what they are trying to make the focus of the conversation.

Get a life, fucker! Well, you don't always need to use the word fucker. And sometimes it's wise not to. Why? Because when you attack back, you don't want to sound too aggressive, for it can communicate insecurity. Your attack needs to be calm yet strong. Make it too aggressive and you will sound insecure and give the bully a chance to get back at you. Calm and strong; that's it. However, calm doesn't mean timid. Calm means a fair demonstration of confidence. To elaborate on this point...

YOUR LOOK AND VOICE MATTER.

Most of the communication is nonverbal. That's not to say that words, in and of themselves, are not powerful. It's just that communication is too complex a process to be done only through words.

We are emotional beings and we express our emotions using our voice. In fact, the first method we use to communicate and express our needs is voice. Babies cry and make noise. First, they cry and make angry voices usually to get their needs met (by the way, this is not the best way to communicate as an adult despite the fact that some adults still use it!). Then they learn to laugh and make happy noises. And we all have the ability to dictate what emotion is being communicated through the tone of voice.

And then come facial expressions. Emotions show themselves on our faces; and as if it was a universal language, we almost all can understand the facial expressions of happiness, sadness, anger, fear, and disgust.

When dealing with someone who is pushing your boundaries or is trying to bully you, your mindset is important but so are your facial expressions and tone of voice. And sometimes, they are all you need to make someone stop being a dick.

Predators and animals are very good at demonstrating this. If you step on a cat's tail, it will use its voice in an aggressive manner, make unwelcoming (even angry) facial expressions, and expand its body to hold as much space as it can as a demonstration of power and dominance. And many animals do this before they fight. Those are like warning signs. What's being sub-communicating is, "Back off! I will fuck you up should you proceed doing what you are doing". And this is exactly what you need to be communicating through your voice, facial expressions, and even body language.

Well, calm down, you tiger. We, humans, of course, have to do this in a civilized manner. You are not a fucking cat!

To civilize it, let's get back to the purpose of why we are doing this. Our purpose is to communicate in a dominant manner when someone steps on our tail or crosses the line. To stand up to tyrannies. Why? To protect ourselves from getting our rights violated or boundaries crossed. Even to get our needs/rights back should they be taken away from us unjustly or oppressively. See, dominance isn't a bad thing if you think about it this way. It's even necessary; psychologically and morally necessary.

Is there a specific voice tone or facial expressions to communicate that?

Not exactly because social situations are contextual and too complex.

But let's talk about the basics. You do want to have a firm look. That means firm eye contact that is a bit aggressive. That means a) eye contact that lasts way more than what's friendly. b) a negative (but threatening) emotion such as anger or disgust expressed on your face. Remember that we all can recognize such emotions in people's faces, so the other person will recognize it. Again, the purpose of communicating this emotion is to give a warning sign. This means that you have to be willing to get involved in some kind of conflict. The conflict may include enforcing your boundaries and refusing a specific type of treatment. Basically, standing up for yourself. Anyway, you shouldn't be afraid of conflict. And you shouldn't avoid it in such cases where you boundaries are being pushed.

The same goes for the voice. Firm. Loud if it's necessary. Scolding if needed. You're not talking to the love of your life; you're talking to an enemy.

By that, you are communicating the idea that you have teeth and you are willing to use them. You are willing to stand up for yourself. Of course, you cannot do that only by words. And sometimes you can do it only through your facial expression and tone of voice, regardless of the words. So, leverage that. It's one technique that you can use along with other techniques when you have to.

PART TWO

This part deals with the manipulative behavior of toxic people.

By reading it, you will have an idea of what tricks toxic people use, the motives behind them, and how to handle such tricks and toxicity.

GASLIGHTING 101

Can you trust your memory?

According to some scientific resources, and my own shitty experiences, I can tell you: not really. Our memory isn't as reliable as we think. It's full of gaps that we end up filling biasedly and incorrectly.

And this might surprise a lot of people. But the main purpose of memory isn't to remember; it's to learn from the past. Therefore, it's highly subjective and can be as biased as our feelings and thoughts and beliefs are.

And toxic people take advantage of this piece of information.

They mess with your memory and fill the gaps to make you

believe what serves their agendas. They alter your sense of reality by questioning it. And that's, dear reader, is what we call gaslighting. Regardless of the origin of the word, which is an old movie, gaslighting is a manipulation tactic. And it's very destructive if you are not careful enough. Not only will it make you do and believe what they want, but it also makes you question yourself and believe you are crazy, forgetful, making things up, and plain an idiot. It's one of these tactics that can directly damage your self-esteem in addition to manipulating you.

First of all, you need to develop your ability to spot gaslighting. It's not that hard if you pay attention. You just need to pay attention to the right things. Once you are able to spot gaslighting, and you can see things for what they really are, you have your power back and you can do something about the situation.

One of these things is a person who is consistently disappointing others. But almost always has a justification. I am not saying that all unreliable people are gaslighters. Some are just lazy and, well, unreliable! What I'm saying is, there's a specific type of unreliable people who are more likely to use gaslighting. First of all, reliable people don't need to use gaslighting. But if I'm unreliable, I may use gaslighting from time to time *if* I want to avoid taking the responsibility for my behavior. And guess who likes to avoid taking responsibility and accountability? That's right. Toxic people. Mostly narcissists, but toxic people in general.

A consistent pattern of lying is an obvious sign. Lie, is shouldn't even be mentioning this, but here we go. I believe that gaslighting is an advanced level of lying. In this case, the lie is about altering reality or about altering the past that you know to be true. This alteration serves their goals and agendas. They will say they never said that. Or that they meant X when they said Y, even though at the moment they meant Z and you both know it. Or they will tell you, or give you hints, that you are overreacting to one of their (shitty) actions.

But the trick is that you end up believing that! And it's hard to tell why.

Talking about too many topics and details can be a subtle gaslighting strategy. It's a distraction strategy to make you too confused to focus on their lie and spot it. That's something to be aware of. Make them cut to the chase and don't lose your focus.

One last thing to watch for is their refusal to be held accountable. They hate boundaries, and they shy away from taking responsibility. Again, that's why most narcissists are also gaslighters.

Once you discover that someone is gaslighting you, and that's actually the harder part, you need to have a different strategy for dealing with them. They are not operating on values such as honesty and telling the truth. They are concealing truths and are trying to twist reality to get what they want. And, this is the big part, they are refusing to take responsibility for one of their actions and are manipulating you either to let it slide and not hold them accountable or to take responsibility for it instead of them.

Those are the hidden agendas most of the time.

So, how do you deal with such agendas and behaviors?

Don't give them what they want, which is the relinquishment of responsibility. Don't engage with their values, which are dishonesty and concealing truths. You engage in them when you "enable" them to get away with what they did and "excuse" them. Hold them accountable.

Here's more practical advice.

Guard your memory. One of the ways you can do this is by documenting things. I am serious! In professional settings, keep everything tracked and documented in an official way. Losing track of that might make it hard to remember who did what and when and how or what was really said, done, and decided. That's not a loophole you want to overlook. In your personal life, you can do a version of that, too. It can be writing how things made you feel and which behavior made you feel what. Of course, it's a reminder to yourself and not to go and show them what you have written (unless you want to). But it's more about your own sanity and knowing the truth for yourself. Then acting on this truth to protect yourself against lying. Journaling, too, can be helpful to some extent to document what happened and how it happened. But you need to integrate it with the next piece of advice.

Trust your perspective. We said that gaslighters have the skill of altering your sense of reality. They make you doubt your own judgment. Heck, they persuade you against your better judgment. So, how do you handle such situations and manipulation? Well, partly, by trusting your own perspective. And by disregarding theirs. That might sound a bit selfish. But fuck it. If most of the time they are right and you excuse them and they end up taking so little responsibility compared to you, then something is going on. Something fishy is going on. And you need to trust your perspective and discard theirs. Let me clarify what I mean by the word 'perspective' so that I don't lead you astray as they do.

According to the dictionary, perspective is a particular attitude towards or way of regarding something; a point of view. Surprise, surprise! Your perspective is your own opinion of reality. In the case of gaslighting, this opinion is being shut down and shaped to disserve you. So, if your opinion is always wrong, challenged, or shaped, you need to take a stand. If the reality is always against your opinion, something is wrong. And you need to listen to your own opinion and thus have your own perspective and then trust it, for god's sake.

Some people are easily gaslighted because they don't trust their own opinions or are easily talked out of believing them. That can be the case for various reasons such as low self-worth or doubts or being biased or having some kind of wishful thinking. And sometimes the manipulation is just so damn good.

So, dealing with gaslighting is first about recognizing it for what it really is. Then, you should take actions to prevent it from affecting you. You do that by guarding your memory and trusting your perspective. From there, you should start setting some clear boundaries and asserting them. For instance, a certain way of treatment that you will no longer excuse or accept their justification when it comes to it. Do keep in mind, however, that once you set boundaries and start holding them accountable, the rage will surface. And it can be dangerous to deal with the gaslighter depending on what type of person they are. But do expect some tension and rage. Other manipulation tactics might be thrown at your face, and maybe even actual objects. So, be careful and cautious. Protect yourself. I am not saying you should shy away from conflict or avoid it. It's sometimes necessary and the right thing to do. But do keep in mind what might happen when you expose a gaslighter and when you block their way to where they want to go. Rage. It shouldn't scare you; it should just make you prepared.

Setting clear boundaries and walking away are the best next steps. That might not be as easy as it sounds, but it's important. Losing a gaslighter is never a loss; it's a sign you can't put up with their shit, and that's a compliment.

UNERSTANDING AND HANDLING SILENT TREATMENT

The silent treatment is bloody toxic. And so is the guilt-tripping. I personally believe both of them have a lot in common.

To be able to handle them, you need to understand what guides them. More specifically, what the other person is trying to achieve by using them. Once you have an idea what that is, you can choose a course of action that serves and protects you.

The silent treatment is a manipulation tactic. And almost all manipulation tactics have one underlying goal. The other person is trying to have more power than you so that you do what they want. Manipulation tactics are the leverage tools they use to achieve their goals. Those tactics are supposed to shake the power balance and tilt it a bit towards their side. He who has more power will have more options and resources.

Of course, this is a shitty way to manage relationships. Healthy relationships should be pronounced by fairness and justice. But evil exists! Shit happens. And manipulation can work.

Don't make it work against you and nip this shit in the bud. How? They can't take power from you; you give it to them. Well, they manipulate you to give it to them. Realize what power they trying to gain or leverage and hoard it.

The silent treatment manipulation is about deprivation and uncertainty and taking validation away. Those feelings are unbearable. We would do anything to get something valuable back or to ease feelings of uncertainty. That's the power they want.

And you give it to them once you take an action. Don't take any action to handle the silent treatment. I repeat. The way you handle the silent treatment is by simply doing *nothing* at all. Just watch and observe. See, the whole purpose of using the silent treatment is to make you take a certain action. Don't. If you don't, the power will remain as it is and maybe tilt a bit towards your side. Face their silence with equal silence. Face their inertia with similar inertia. Get busy doing something meaningful and ignore them. Then watch them get more furious.

The sub-communication goes something like this: you are being a dick in a silent way to make me do something. Fuck that! Grow the fuck up and communicate as an adult or remain as you are. And I am not doing it for you!

Given that that thing is important to them, they should, at least, change the tactic. And even if they didn't, by not doing anything at all you are refusing to play a toxic, childish game that is meaningless and immature. Either way, the power balance is intact. You didn't lose your power to them. And that's what's important.

But wait! If you do care about the person for whatever

reason, then you might consider changing the way you handle this.

Confrontation. Period!

Face them and ask directly what's going on. They are acting in a passive-aggressive way. Why is that? They might deny. Stand your ground and insist on getting an answer. They might be unaware of their behavior, so you need to highlight it in an assertive manner. Whatever you do, insist and face them with the reality of their behavior. The alternative is that you will get involved in a toxic interaction with them where there's passive aggression underneath the surface. Who wants that, especially with someone they care about?

In simple words, confront and make them come to see the passive aggression they are harboring. And help them express it, for god's sake. You care about them, don't you?

If you don't care about them, just do nothing. Ignore. Ignore while being aware of the dynamics of wanting to shift the power balance for selfish gains. It's amusing to watch such drama.

RECLAIM YOUR INDEPENDENCE

Dependence isn't a bad word. Overdependence is. Independence is not a bad word, too. It becomes bad when it's an obsession that's driven by fear. And *interdependence* is an amazing word that we don't talk about that often.

That said, the struggle between dependence and independence can be used to destroy characters and control people.

One of the malicious ways to control someone is by making them resourceless. And then making sure you are the source of what they need.

This way you can rest assured they won't leave even if they want to (because they can't). You will rest assured they will do as you wish because they can't make their own decisions.

They might be dependent on you financially or emotionally or in any other way. They are overdependent on you, and they need you.

Some people have issues with independence and want someone to be their cornerstone. Other people want to feel needed and important. Both make a nice mix. Both can go from an end to the other quite surprisingly and indiscriminately. The ones who want to feel needed usually work, consciously or subconsciously, on destroying the other party's independence as much as their ego fancies and as much as the other person will allow them to.

And some people don't actually have issues with independence but meet someone who can crack that. They slowly start sacrificing their independence and become *overly* dependent on whatever they are getting from that person. And that person might be aware of what they are doing or not. They could have malicious intents or not. But the damage is done anyway.

A classic example is the parent who overprotects their children, even as adults. They work on solving their problems, providing them with what they need, and never "allowing" them to have new experiences. This might be done with good intentions, but it's damaging. They become overdependent on their parents and can't create their own independence. And here we have infant adults who resent their parents and who are resented by their parents as well.

Another painful example is the spouse who makes their partner dependent on them financially, so that they remain in control. Or the boyfriend who doesn't allow his girlfriend to solve her problems by herself. Or the girlfriend who conveys to her boyfriend the idea that no one will accept and love him but her.

You have to be careful of anyone who tries to *overly* limit the "domain" of your independence. And you have to be careful of any relationship that has the dynamic of making you overdependent on someone/something. Healthy relationships foster independence and ultimately lead to interdependence, which is different.

As a reminder, it might be you who is tilting towards dependence and moving away from independence. And that's not a wise thing to do. And it could be that the other person is a master manipulator who is messing with the balance of power in the relationship by making you overdependent. Or it could be both!

Either way, reclaim your independence. An entire book can be written about how to do that, but one of the quickest ways is to realize what dependence is costing you. And slowly but surely build your own independence by investing in yourself. Give yourself the things that you desperately want others to give you.

Be aware, however, that you will probably upset that person on whom you are dependent. They might even try to sabotage your efforts to be independent. Well, what do you need to see more than this? This's a surefire sign you *must* be independent and free from that person and then see if the relationship makes sense anymore. Don't let them stop you and don't be afraid of getting into fights and conflicts, for that's a necessary sacrifice to reclaim things so valuable you'll grow resentful without: your independence and power.

DON'T TRY TO PROVE ANYTHING TO THEM. EVER!

We are social creatures. To some extent, and to varying degrees, we care about our position in society. Therefore, we care about validation and approval, especially from those we care about. Nobody can live if everybody around them is disgusted at the sight of them. That's isolation and alienation.

But on the other hand, it becomes dangerous if you're over-dependent on that validation and approval. It becomes dangerous when everything you do is an attempt to get approval and validation from those around you, even if they don't like you. It means that you took your natural need for social connection and acceptance to an extreme and allowed it to control you.

That's a weakness of character. A flaw. A deadweight. People who try to prove their worth to others and impress them aren't living their lives in honest ways.

Some of us develop this flaw as a result of our upbringing. You know, do everything right and don't upset anyone. The message here is that other people's opinions and approval are *more* important than yours. More specifically, *their* opinions of you are more important than yours about yourself.

And off we go, trying to please everyone and get their approval! Trying to *prove* to others that we are worthy or smart or pretty or successful or whatever. We often do that by overspending or pretending or overcompensating, to mention only a few.

Now, just as sharks go to where there's blood to prey on some victim, some toxic people are able to recognize this 'flaw' and exploit it. And some are even good at manipulating you and provoking it.

They know about your hunger to get approval or to prove something, and they give you that. Sometimes! Usually to make you do something for them. That's manipulation and dishonesty. And sometimes they deprive you of that and keep you trying to prove something to them. That not only feeds their ego but it's also a good manipulation tool to make you do what they want.

In both cases, you consider their approval important and that you have to prove something to them. Well, we need to start here. Maybe it's just your need for validation and acceptance being exploited and used because there's a wound right there. And maybe when you relook at that need in a healthier way, you would value your own opinion and approval instead of theirs. Like, you don't need it, and you're fine without it. You're fine if they disagree with you or even dislike you. seriously! Try it. you would be amazed how little their opinions and approval have on your life. And when it comes to their opinions of you and their approval, your own opinions of yourself and how you live your life should always win. Even if you care about them deeply. Let alone if they're just toxic people who are just trying to exploit you. Your opinions and approval of yourself should matter more than the opinions and approval of everybody else combined.

This way, toxic people won't find this weak spot in your psyche and hijack it. Think about it. You genuinely *don't* care about proving anything to anyone. They have nothing to work on. There's no blood because the wound no longer bleeds.

Become aware of this emotional flaw and work on it. It's not something to be ashamed of. It's something a lot of us struggle with, especially in the era of social media. And it's not only about handling toxic people. When you have this mindset of valuing your own opinions and not seeking approval to feel worthy, it will benefit you in many areas of your life. In my own opinion, you will start living your most honest life. Why? Because you will start listening to your own voice and your own conscience. And they do tell you useful things about how you should be in the world if you are willing to really listen to them. If you build a life around the other noisy voices of everybody around you and the nagging voices of your inner critic, regret is your final destination. Avoiding the sound of your conscience is a recipe for being corrupted. It's a surefire way to live a life that's not your own and that's not any good for you either.

So, again, this is not just about toxic people and I am starting to steer away from the main topic of this book. But it's okay. I want to give you a deeper understanding of this idea because I do want to shift your mindset and not just your behavior. It's not about not caring about what people think of you; it's about not allowing your need for approval to corrupt you; it's about caring more about living *your* own life instead of wasting it to make people who don't even think about you that often, let alone like you, happy!

PART THREE

This part touches on deeper topics that mostly have nothing to do with toxic people themselves. The ideas and topics that are about your own behavior and mentality. If you know all there is about toxic people but ignore the following points, you will still suffer. Those points should help you become more resilient in the face of hurt, pain, and malevolence.

TAKE OFF YOUR ROSE-EYED GLASSES AND DON'T IGNORE THE RED FLAGS

The term 'red flags' is usually used in dating materials. But it can apply to *any* type of relationship. You can call them warning signs. Stuff that will make the interactions unhealthy and hurtful.

And here's an interesting fact: toxic people give you plenty of warning signs, whether intentionally or not. Largely that's because no one can hide their true behavior forever, and it will often manifest itself in smaller situations and on smaller scales. But it will reveal itself. You just have to pay attention.

We don't pay attention because we are either biased or plain naïve. Or both! In romantic cases, we are biased because of the chemicals that are running through our minds and blinding us. But generally, we are biased because we believe there's something good about this relationship and this person/these people. And we don't want to shake that belief. We want to maintain that false image we have in our minds about the reality instead of confronting and accepting and challenging it.

While there's no one comprehensive list for red flags, most of the time we are aware when there's something fishy in the air. The so-called 'gut feeling' kicks in and our conscience takes over.

As I said, people are consistently telling you who they are. You just have to pay attention. And pay attention to actions, not to words.

Of course, I don't mean that you should go out there and beat people to death for their mistakes. We all make mistakes and come short every now and then. What I mean is, address what bothers you. Don't ignore it. Especially in new relationships. Don't overuse compassion to the point of enabling someone else to act delinquently towards you.

Red flags can be unintended mistakes. Or they can be a pattern of behavior the other person has. It takes communication to address the first type. And for the other type, it takes a serious examination to know whether you are to tolerate that kind of behavior or not, then a dose of communication.

Either way, keep an open eye. Don't be biassed, and don't ignore red flags. Don't rationalize them. And actually, if you listen to the *quiet* voice of your conscience, maybe it will have a valuable opinion about what you should do. Maybe that's what you should do because it's quite painful to ignore the red flags even though you are aware of them and then get hurt by them, understanding that you have known it all the time but have chosen to ignore it. That's quite painful. I know that from personal experience.

SOMETIMES, YOU NEED TO GROW BIGGER.

Carl Jung once beautifully described how some problems don't have actual or practical solutions. You cannot apply any type of solution to these problems and expect them to go away. They are here to stay. You simply cannot fix or *solve* them.

Discouraging, isn't it?

Wait. Jung didn't stop here. He suggested a way to handle such problems.

The only 'solution' to these types of problems is to *outgrow them*. To become bigger than them. To become so big that those problems don't bother you anymore.

You don't actively work on solving the problem because, let's face it, there's no practical solution under the sun. Instead, you work on yourself to become bigger and outgrow the problem. One way to look at it is that you work on the parts of yourself that are affected by the problem and make them stronger. Or that you work on yourself generally so that the problem seems trivial compared to who you are now. And I think there are more ways to look at the statement: outgrow the problem so that it doesn't hurt you anymore. But the point remains. You grow bigger.

The alternative is that you get smaller compared to the problem. That happens when it cripples you. They cripple you because they are perpetual; since there's no practical solution to these types of problems, focusing on them can be one of the ways you grow smaller compared to them. You will always end up disappointed and powerless because of the lack of the possibility of the solution and the presence of pain.

That's not a good option. I prefer the option of outgrowing that shit.

You outgrow a problem in many ways. However, all of them have one thing in common: you become bigger and better. That can happen by becoming more self-aware, developing more self-respect, establishing your independence, achieving a certain level of success, developing certain skills, or creating a certain lifestyle.

In Eminem's words in his song with Sia *Beautiful Pain*, ". . . and tomorrow you may even feel so good that you're willing to forgive them even after all the shit you've been put through, this feeling of resilience is building."

You see where this is getting at, don't you? And no, I am not asking you to forgive anyone now. I am just making the point that you should outgrow any perpetual problem that has no practical solution and therefore not get affected by it anymore. Then, decide if you want to forgive or not. Now, focus on growing. Now, don't focus on the problem itself because if you do, you will get smaller.

When it comes to toxic people, I think that you now understand that your troubled relationships with some of them belong to this category of problems you need to outgrow.

Focusing on the relationship itself won't help. Focusing on how to fix the problems won't help. Hell, focusing on the toxic behavior of the other person/people won't help. And obviously, focusing on fixing or changing the other party won't work or help or even make sense.

This can apply to your relationship with your family if you believe it's toxic; who cares if you had a toxic family if you are leading a meaningful life that you deeply enjoy? Or that toxic narcissistic friend who makes you feel small and useless; you could grow to the point of not feeling small in comparison to them. By the way, narcissists make you feel insignificant because they subconsciously remind you of all the ways you are neglecting yourself when you see them. Or that abuse you went through; you cannot undo it, but you are now a stronger and wiser person who leads a good life.

Every case is different. The problems you need to outgrow will differ from the ones I need to outgrow. The ways you outgrow your problem will be as unique as your finger-prints; similar to mines in their very nature, yet different in how they manifest themselves in the world. Figure this out by yourself, but generally realize that you need to grow. If you throw a chair at a baby, that poor baby might die. But if you throw it at a strong healthy adult, it won't hurt them. Yet, it's the same chair and the same hit. The hit and the existence of the chair (reads pain!) are inevitable and irreversible; it's the strength of the individual in each case that differs.

To wrap this up, outgrow your toxic relationships with toxic people instead of dwelling on how miserable or toxic they are/*were*. You will give them power by dwelling on them. This is probably the case with hurtful relationships that are close to you such as family members or intimate relationships. See how you should grow and do it. The benefits are limitless and there's no downside. And by the way, this incredible piece of advice by Carl Jung can be used in a variety of situations, not just dealing with toxic people and relationships. So, make use of it.

REALIZE THAT YOU DON'T ALWAYS HAVE TO QUESTION YOURSELF BECAUSE OF THEIR ACTIONS.

There's this quote that I find fascinating. It goes, "If you don't heal what hurt you, you will bleed on people who didn't cut you."

I am not here to justify the toxic behavior. I am here to make the point that most of the toxic behavior is not about you at all. It's about wounds people have they haven't healed.

When we are hurt by toxic people, we sometimes have the tendency to scan ourselves for flaws and mistakes and weaknesses. We tend to blame ourselves and play the role of a harsh judge, usually with the good intentions to set things right or the bad intentions of secretly looking down at ourselves.

We think that we are flawed when we get hurt. Or that it must be because we misbehaved some way or another.

But that's not always the truest conclusion we can draw.

What if it has nothing to do with us? What if we don't even have to question ourselves? And what if it was only because of wounds the other person has? At least, in the largest part.

What if the blood you are seeing isn't yours? You would be trying to heal wounds that don't exist. And you would exaggerate the blood flow of some of your wounds. Or worse, you would open up wounds that aren't bleeding and make them hurt all over again. In the name of what? In the name of trying to figure out what you did wrong/why someone hurt you.

Maybe that's the flaw you have to work on: being too harsh on yourself and taking too much responsibility than what's healthy. Questioning yourself and internalizing the abuse as it's a sign of your shortcomings.

Remind yourself that maybe the blood you are seeing isn't yours.

They hurt you because they are hurting. I can regretfully confess that I did hurt some people and mistreated them just because I was already hurting because of something that had nothing to do with them. So, think about it. What if this 'something' was trauma or a deeper psychological issue and you just happened to be in the wrong place at the wrong time?

Of course, I am suggesting that you should excuse the toxic behavior just because it's not about you. But do realize that since it's not because of you, you don't have to question yourself because of it. Don't take it personally. Don't let it get to your heart. The practical way you 'don't take it personally' is actually about reminding yourself that you don't have to question yourself because of it. It's their wounds, not your shortcomings.

This doesn't mean you shouldn't stand up for yourself. But with this mindset, you will feel stronger and more understanding. You can't control how a person feels about themselves and the world. That's their issue and it shouldn't dictate how you feel about yourself and the world. Equally, it shouldn't mean they can get away with anything just because they feel bad. There's a balance there between the wisdom that stems from empathy and the strength that stems from setting boundaries. Watch out who is bleeding; it doesn't always have to be you, and it doesn't always have to be about you.

WALK AWAY AND LEAVE.

Well, it's not that simple. It's not obvious when you should leave. And even if it is, how you do it can be problematic, let alone emotionally complicated.

I understand that this piece of advice is given a lot when dealing with toxic people. But it's often not broken down and explained. To break it down, we need to look at its two levels.

First, realizing that you should walk away. It's not always easy to figure out when to walk away. It may seem easy and obvious for someone who is observing from a distance. But for someone who is tangled up in a toxic dynamic, things aren't that straightforward. They are usually emotionally complicated.

Even if you realize it's a toxic dynamic, it's not evident that people will simply walk away thanks to this realization. Think of all the stories of people who stay in bad relationships because "the devil you know is better than the one you don't." And this brings us to the second part.

Second, actually walking away. There are many ways you

can walk away from someone or a group of people. Some are harder to implement than others. Some are necessary only in specific cases. And some are necessary regardless of the situation. It's complicated because social settings and relationships are complicated. But, however you do it, it's necessary; if you are absolutely convinced that you should walk away but still not do it, more pain will find its way to your life.

Let's start with the part about when to walk away.

Well, you just happened to be reading a book that explained a lot of toxic people's behaviors, patterns, and mindsets. Many of these signs and patterns are manifesting themselves in a certain person/social interaction? It's time.

Some of the advice in this book was about your own behavior. They are supposed to make you an emotionally healthier person. The idea is that once you are emotionally healthy, you will be able to recognize what's unhealthy. And once you deem something as unhealthy, it's time you picked your things and left. Else, you will get hurt by it.

Some people are toxic to you. They enjoy seeing you suffer. Some are toxic to others, and you should be careful that one day you might be one of those 'others.' Some are toxic to themselves and have shitty lives. They are full of anger and resentment and don't wish anyone well. They will drag you down should you hang around them. Some are evil; some are just scared and hopeless. And maybe some are all of that in one peculiar package!

I hope that by reading this far you have honed your ability to spot toxicity and delinquent behaviors. With this ability, it becomes easier to know *when* to walk away. As soon as something isn't as healthy as you want it to be, and you do want it to be healthy because you are healthy/getting healthier, you know you should walk away.

But *how* to actually walk away?

That's a tricky question. Sometimes people ask it and they genuinely don't know how to get themselves out of a terrible situation. Some toxic people are evil and can use their resources and power to keep you stuck. To deny that this can happen is irresponsible and unrealistic. In this case, professional help is very, very needed. You need someone who is professional and who is on your side and wishes you good.

On the other hand, some people ask this question as a lame excuse for their laziness or cowardice. They know how. Maybe they are convinced there is pain and toxicity and drama because of this person/these people. Like, they know they should walk away. And, again, for them, it's not a question of ability. It's as simple as picking their things and leave. It's as straightforward as confronting that person. It's not that they can't; it's that they are afraid and unwilling. They are avoiding conflict. They value the status quo and comfort over truth and authenticity.

To put it brutally and honestly, they don't want to take the responsibility for taking themselves out of a terrible situation. It's a new and demanding type of responsibility. And it will alter their lives in many ways they are not ready for. And hey, the devil you know is better than the one you don't. Because even if they walked away, what would they do next? They haven't got a clue. And for them, this type of uncertainty outweighs the pain of staying.

So, it's the fear of actually doing it and/or the fear of what comes next after doing it. It's not the actual actions they need to take in order to leave. Many things in life seem paralyzing not because of the complicity of the actions we need to take, but because of the emotional complicity of taking these actions. And this emotional complicity is where we need to look.

Be honest with yourself and see which category you belong to. And, please, leave your ego at the door for now. It's not the right time to be blinded by the idea of being too cool to be an idiot or even an actual victim (when I say a victim, I am talking about the case in which people are actually and technically stuck. That can happen, and there's no shame in being a victim. There's a difference between an actual victim and someone who plays the role of the victim. But that's a long discussion that we can have elsewhere)..

That said, here's what walking away is in a nutshell. Leaving and walking away are about *setting boundaries*. Sometimes the boundary means that this person can no longer be in your life anymore in any possible way. A total cut off with zero contact. You take your things, say goodbye (or fuck you!), and leave. And sometimes the boundary means keeping this person at bay and minimizing contact to a certain degree. But anyway, it's a boundary that you set and defend; a decision that you make and stand behind. The actual context of the boundary is irrelevant to the fact that you have to set it. It depends on the situation and the facts.

If it's technically hard to leave for good, it's still possible to walk away because it's always possible to set a new boundary. This is good news. For instance, I have some people who I totally cut off from my life. For good. And others who are still somehow in my life, but they understand which lines they shouldn't cross or what I will not tolerate and put up with. Usually, the reason they are still in my life is that they are people I currently have to come in contact with a lot, like family members or co-workers. The point is that I decided that those relationships with those people are doing me more harm than good. They are toxic. Some are abusive. And I just don't want that. So, I will do whatever it takes to let them go. Even if they are family members. I do realize how hard and complicated this can be, but what's the alternative? The pain that got you to get this book and read this far; the demise of your life and emotional sanity. That's not a cheap price to pay. And if you think it's a cheap one to pay for the sake of saving your relationships with these people, then fuck you, you haven't learned anything from this book. Ask for a refund or read it one more time without your rosy-eyed glasses. I do care about every reader, but I am willing to let you go should you choose to stick to your old delinquent ways of being. And that's exactly what you should do with those people in your life if you are serious about this.

I don't have anything more to say about leaving and walking away. I feel like I will just be repeating the same ideas and concepts. Will repeating them make you get up and do it? I don't know. But, here's a quick summary of what you should do to leave:

- Have a nose for toxicity.

- Recognize it and spot it.

- If you found a lot of the signs and behaviors and mentalities we talked about it in this book, that's something. Don't ignore it.

- Do whatever it takes to leave and walk the fuck away. You do that quite literally or by setting clear, strong boundaries. Either case, you know deep within you that this relationship doesn't serve you anymore and actually hurts you. This realization is important to push you away and to keep you aiming at healthy people and relationships.

In the end, maybe you deserve better.

PART FOUR

B elow you will find 17 short tips that have one goal
in mind: to help you communicate in healthy and
better ways.

By doing that, you are making yourself a slightly better
communicator who is emotionally secure. Communicating in this way will increase your chances of getting a
proper response from those around you. It will also help
you weed out the ones who don't like to communicate in
honest and healthy ways. Lastly, you will be able, with the
help of these 17 tips, to set boundaries and express your
needs in better ways.

So, think of the previous parts of the book as ways to
destroy toxic and unhealthy relationships and to get away
from them. And think of this part as a way to move towards healthy relationships that are based on respect and
honesty and assertiveness.

EXPRESS YOUR POSITIVE
NEEDS USING "I"

When people feel attacked and criticized, they will naturally get defensive. Shutdown, even.

It is hard to have any conversation when the person in front of you thinks of you as threatening. They will hardly accept your input, and they will give very little output.

So, we have to do something different.

It is usually about your needs. You are trying to get one of your needs met. Make that the focus: your needs. More specifically, your positive needs. And avoid making the focus the other person flaws and mistakes as much as possible.

"I like to spend more time with you." Instead of "you never have any time for me!"

"I would like to spend some time alone." Instead of "you always interfere with my own business."

"I would appreciate if you come on time." Instead of "you are always late." Or, worse, "you are such a lazy person! You will never learn responsibility."

Use "I" and focus on your positive need. Avoid using "you" and the generalizations such as *always* and *never*.

USE THE "L.U.E"

Here is what that stands for:

- **L**isten
- **U**nderstand
- **E**mphasize

Drop everything. Focus. Be mentally present.

The other person has something to say, and they deserve to be heard. You know you feel good when someone listens to you, don't you?

You listen to understand. You don't assume you do.

While you are listening, you eliminate the desire to judge, to come up with awesome and clever replies, and to defend yourself (Extremely important, even if the other person sounded threatening).

You listen to understand where they are coming from. Even if you don't agree with them.

But understanding isn't always enough. You need to level up and emphasize.

Understanding is intellectual. Emphasizing is emotional.

When you emphasize with someone, you kind of feel what they are feeling. Quite literally. You mirror them in every way that you end up having a clue about what they are feeling, which helps you connect on a deeper level. On an emotional level.

Some people have this natural gift of emphasizing with people. The rest of us have to work on developing it.

When people feel heard, understood both intellectually and emotionally, deeper connections can develop. Deeper than you could imagine.

READ THE ATMOSPHERE BEFORE YOU SPEAK

Here is a pro tip.

Before you speak to a group of people, or to one person, try to gauge what those people are/this person is feeling.

This will help you deliver your message more efficiently.

If you notice that your friend is tired, emotionally

drained, and just feeling blue, maybe this is not a good time to tell a joke. Maybe it isn't a good time to discuss something important.

If you walk into a room and notice that the people there are happy, then maybe it is a good time to ask them for something. Or to discuss something with them.

If you notice that your friend is not quite listening, maybe it is time he went, for he might be late to something. Or just tired.

In short, make sure it is the right time. Do that partly by gauging the general feelings the other person is probably feeling.

Don't be the creepy guy who cracks a joke at funerals!

SAY NO

When you don't want to do something, say no.

When it is going to cost you a lot, say no.

If you don't say no in such situations, you will hurt yourself.

And you are not saying yes because you want to or because you genuinely want to help the other person. You are saying yes because you don't want to upset that person. So, you upset yourself.

Say yes only when you mean it.

It is not wrong to say no when it is too much. Standing up for yourself is one of the best things you can do.

You can justify why you said no, or you can just leave it like that. But say it. Especially if you are not used to saying it. Especially if you always say yes. Especially if you are resentful and angry toward a lot of things and people.

This will make you a better person because you will treat yourself better. And people respect and trust people who stand up for themselves this way.

YOU ARE NOT A VICTIM, SO DON'T ACT LIKE ONE

It is understandable to seek social support when you are down.

But here is something to keep in mind: don't play the victim role.

Playing the victim role is about refusing to accept the responsibility for your life. Usually by blaming everything around you. And then by going around trying to prove that life is unfair and that every possible solution, offered to you by others, is useless and that you are a hopeless case.

You do that to get sympathy and attention and care. You can do that by complaining. Or dramatic social media posts. Or by being extra pessimistic and cynical. Or by just hopelessly laying there watching your life deteriorating and doing nothing about that.

You can do something. But you don't. and you know that. And people also know it and see through your excuses. You are after sympathy and someone solving all this shit for you. You don't want to get your hands dirty.

People will neither trust nor respect you. They will perceive you as weak, and no wonder! You present yourself as a weak person who is oppressed and helpless. You will miss a lot of chances that could help you become better because people won't offer them to you in the first place because they know you will just whine and get lazy.

Like it or hate it, communicating to people that you are a victim will get you to a worse place, despite the immediate, short-term gains.

Resist the urge to be pessimistic and complain. If it is so hard, do it with people you completely trust, and even then, don't overdo it.

ARE YOU AN INTROVERT OR AN EXTROVERT?

Extraversion is one of the big five.

The big five is a theory that has five measures for personality. And it is, by far, the most accurate theory (unlike the Myers).

People who are high on extraversion thrive on social interactions. They get their energy from interacting with people. Jobs that tie them to desks and offer minimal social contact can drive them crazy if most of their time is spent there.

People low on extraversion, introverts, get drained from social interactions quite quickly. Their inner world is usually captivating and consumes a lot of their energy. Jobs that require them to interact with people intensely can drive them crazy if they don't find ways to recharge their energy.

And sure, we have people who don't score high on either end. They score in between, usually orienting toward one end more than the other.

It is not that extroverts are needy and introverts are anti-social. It is all about energy consumption.

Try to understand where you score on this extraversion measure. Then align your social interactions based on this. This way, you are playing on your strength. And it would be extra nice if you could figure out where do the people you care about the most score, too, so you can interact with them in a way that aligns with their personality.

YOU DON'T ALWAYS HAVE TO RESPOND TO EVERYTHING

And you are not obliged to do that.

Pick your battles carefully.

The goal of social interaction is to maximize your well-being and to help you become a better person.

To reach that goal, sometimes, you need to ignore a lot of things. You don't always have to win arguments, or have your say on everything, or answer every question people ask.

Save your energy for what matters.

DON'T INSULT AND/OR USE SARCASM (UNLESS YOU NEED TO)

Sarcasm is scatological humor. I discussed this in my first book in more depth.

It communicates contempt, resentment, passive aggression, and even disgust.

And no one likes to be called ugly names or be disrespected. People are more sensitive that they appear to be, including you. No one will communicate well when attacked and mocked. You are only building walls between you and hurting the other person in ways that are mean-hearted.

Stop. Don't do it. And don't accept this kind of behavior from anyone. Anyone!

Some tips in this article will help you communicate better. Focus on your positive needs, hold people accountable, and say no. Those are better means to get what you want instead of insulting people. And if what you want is insulting people, then I feel sorry for you.

But there are times during which you need to use sarcasm. It is a sword. And sometimes the only way to stop someone who is using a sword is to use your own sword, to defend yourself or someone else. That is not communication; it is just a way to stand up for yourself.

USE YOUR EYES

There are two aspects here:

- Proper eye contact.
- Showing positive emotions through the eyes.

Proper eye contact is about having a steady look and spending appropriate time looking directly in the eye. You don't want to stare, and you don't want to have a shaky look that lacks focus.

And if you are speaking to a group, make sure you distribute eye contact properly. Generally speaking, divide the audience into groups and spend time looking at every group. Try to explain one idea (sentence) while looking into a group and when you move to the next idea move to the next group.

You need to also realize that the way you look at someone can make a big difference. Just look at how two lovers glance at each other; you can feel their emotions through eye contact alone. Look at how two fighters look at each other before a fight; you can feel the tension and even the hatred burning in their eyes.

In short, eyes can communicate emotions. The way you look can communicate a lot without you saying a word. Pro tip: this can be an excellent way to show love.

Generally speaking, use this to your advantage by summoning positive emotions and looking at someone. Those positive emotions can range from love for this person, love for humans in general, the fact that you want good for this person and so on. Just make sure you stick to proper eye contact so you don't sound creepy, especially if you don't know the other person well enough.

This can go a long way.

BE SLOW TO JUDGE

Slow down. Don't assume anything.

Sometimes, our insecurities take over and make us believe that others don't like us, are plotting against us, are out to get us, and sooner or later they will get rid of us.

Someone doesn't call you back? They don't love you. Someone doesn't reply to you *immediately* on social media? They hate you and they are not real friends. Someone, even if a dear friend, ignores you? He is a shitty person who got himself new friends and forgot about you. Your boss doesn't say Hi? He will fire you.

Hey, take a deep breath.
I am serious. Do it. Take it, and then take another one that's even deeper.

You don't know what is going on inside people's minds. You don't know about their insecurities. Plus, the world doesn't revolve around you.

Take a deep breath again. Believe in yourself. Shut those insecurities down.

When you believe or assume something, your mind will go crazy trying to prove it right. Those assumption usually come from toxic beliefs you have about yourself and about people.

By not trying to prove those assumption true, you are weakening them and therefore weakening the toxic belief itself. And vice versa. Choose wisely what you feed.

MAYBE PEOPLE DON'T UNDERSTAND YOU BECAUSE YOU DON'T UNDERSTAND YOURSELF

I am talking about self-awareness.

I believe that without some amount of self-awareness, you will find it difficult to communicate with people. You cannot even communicate with yourself in an honest way. How on earth will you be able to do that with other people?

You are more likely to hide and try to fake who you are, which we will discuss below. And you will not be able to open up about who you are, your motives, and your values because you have no idea what those are.

Last but not least, without self-awareness, you are more likely to avoid accepting responsibility for your own life. This is a trait which will cost you a lot. And it will make communicating with you painful.

Spend time with yourself. Be honest with yourself. Come to peace with yourself. Then have the guts to be yourself and to express it.

LEARN TO WRITE PROPERLY

I am not talking about developing your writing skills for written communication purposes.

Writing can help you learn how to articulate your thoughts and ideas.

The processes of brainstorming, organizing your ideas, defining the purpose of your writing, and choosing the right words can help you become more articulate.

Those are valuable skills which you need when you are communicating. And this is one of the best ways to develop them.

You don't have to be a world-class writer. Just work on the skills mentioned above and try to produce pieces of writing that are coherent and with ideas presented clearly.

It will take time. And it will help indirectly. But it is fruitful.

ACTING IS EXHAUSTING; THE TRUTH WILL ALWAYS WIN

People can sense authenticity. And they can sense in-authenticity, too.

When you pretend to be something you are not, you may get away with it for a while. But you cannot pretend forever.

And why are you pretending?

Usually, to hide something. A flaw, usually. But you will fail, and people will see it. And when people see it, they will not like that. Not the flaw. They will not like that you tried to hide it because it indicates weakness and avoidance. And because you are too busy hiding it, you are not working on fixing it, which is making it hell a lot worse.

Don't you notice that people who embrace who they are, flaws and all, attract people more. Their behavior indicates that they are strong enough to admit their flaws and not be fazed by it. And also, because they admit it, they are now able to work on improving what can be improved.

Don't hide. People will eventually see your truth. If you are ashamed of it, that is a turn-off. If you are strong enough to embrace it, that is a real demonstration of strong character, and it will manifest itself in your life as self-confidence and resilience.

SOMETIMES, EMOTIONS ARE MORE IMPORTANT THAN LOGIC

"You cannot reason yourself out of something you didn't reason yourself into."

When faced with a difficult situation, or a difficult person, keep in mind that we are emotional beings. And sometimes, our emotions, quite illogical, guide our behaviors.

To persuade someone, or to et along with someone, using logic isn't always the best way. Especially if that person is resisting your attempts.

Slow down. Listen. Understand. Emphasize.

Don't even attempt to change after that; Don't fight emotions and don't deny them; respect and embrace. And realize that sometimes emotions are more important than logic. And that you cannot control people's reactions and emotions.

This can help you understand the weird shit people do sometimes, including your own weird shit. With this understanding, you may handle it better than trying to reason out of it using logic. Most of the communication is about emotions, not logic.

HOLD PEOPLE ACCOUNTABLE FOR THEIR ACTIONS

We talked about communicating using the pronoun "I" and focusing on your positive needs.

The structure goes like:

I + your positive needs

Here, we want to hold people responsible for their actions. That may happen because either they refuse to do that or they hurt us in some way.

We will use the same above structure but add more to it. It goes like this:

I + your positive need + specific thing they did + how it made you feel/impacted you

In extreme cases, it can look like this:

*I + your positive need + specific thing they did + how it made you feel/impacted you + **the consequences of this thing they did on the relationship (in a non-threatening way)***

The order doesn't matter.

This way, it is not criticism and it sounds assertive rather than aggressive.

Here are a few examples:

Between partners: I felt ignored when you weren't here last night. I would love if you could be here when I really need to talk.

Same example but a bit extreme: I felt ignored when you weren't here last night. I would love if you could be here when I really need to talk. If this happened more, it would affect my ability to trust you.

To stand up for yourself: I don't like it when you talk about my friend that way. I would love to spend time with people who respect my friends.

In work: I couldn't reach home early because of the overtime tasks you assigned me to do. I am afraid I can't be late to my family again.

Generally, I would use this technique when I am so upset about what the other person did that I need to address it more than my positive needs; this helps me to handle things right away and not grow resentful.

LEARN HOW TO APOLOGIZE

I heard a quote that describes apologize as not just saying sorry, but more as communicating that you regret doing something specific that hurt the person you are dealing with.

When you apologize about something, be specific.

People say that 'sorry' isn't enough sometimes. I would presume that that is because it is given generally without specifying what you are sorry for.

"I am sorry I made you feel this way." After listening and understanding and emphasizing. This can work like magic given it is genuine.

"I am sorry that I came late and made you wait. That won't happen again." And make sure it doesn't through your actions, which leads me to the second point...

Actions speak louder than words. After you apologize, make sure you not only amend the damage, but also make sure you work hard on not repeating the same mistake again.

Let the other person realize you are trying not to repeat that specific thing you apologized about. Sorry means nothing without actions.

RECOGNIZE WHEN EFFECTIVE COMMUNICATION ISN'T USEFUL

Effective communication isn't magic. It won't always get you what you want. And it won't always work with all people.

And it is OK. At least you know that you are being true to yourself.

The last thing I want to say is, pay attention to how people respond to you when you communicate effectively and honestly. Just make sure you are really honest and are communicating as effectively as possible. This is the litmus test.

Those who respond well, communicate well on their turn, understand and empathize, and apologize if needed, and work to make things better, are the ones who are worth your time. Those are the relationships you should be investing in more.

And those who get defensive, attack you, claim you are sensitive, refuse to apologize, claim to understand while it is obvious that they don't, and show no signs of working to make things better, those are the ones you should cut off. Immediately. Without regrets.

They are not mature enough to handle effective communication and therefore not mature enough to handle healthy relationships.

In the end, maybe you deserve better.

That last line is what I finished the previous part with. And it's what I am finishing this book with. There's no conclusion, for all that you read, but this:

In the end, maybe you deserve better.

Made in the USA
Middletown, DE
09 May 2022